D0984967

THE ARK OF NUH علیه السلام

Quran Stories for Little Hearts

SANIYASNAIN KHAN

Designed and Illustrated by
Achla Anand & Achal K. Anand

Goodword Books Pvt. Ltd.
1, Nizamuddin West Market
New Delhi 110 013
Tel. 435 6666, 435 5454, 435 1128
Fax 9111-435 7333, 435 7980
e-mail: info@goodwordboo¹.s.com

Goodword
FOR KIDS

First published 2002
Reprinted 2002
© Goodword Books 2002

Long, long ago, there lived a pious old man whose name was Noah or Nuh ﷺ. He was a Prophet of Allah. In those days people did not follow the true path. They did not worship Allah. So Allah sent Nuh ﷺ to these people to give them the message of truth. But they all refused to accept his call. He tried his best for a very very long time, but no one, except for a few poor people, paid any heed to him. The rich people turned against Nuh ﷺ and tried to harm him. So he prayed for Allah's help, and Allah heard his prayers and asked him to build an Ark. He told him that a great flood would come which would be a punishment for bad people. So Nuh ﷺ started building a huge Ark with the help of a handful believers. People laughed at them.

When the vessel was ready to sail after lots and lots of hard and tiring work, Nuh عليه السلام asked all the believers to go on board in the name of Allah. Allah told Nuh عليه السلام to bring along a male and a female of every kind of living creature as well. Nuh عليه السلام had to keep enough food to feed them all for a long time. This was a big job, but Nuh عليه السلام and his followers carried it out with all sincerity.

One by one all the animals entered the Ark. Some had wings and some had legs; some crawled and some hopped. All came right into the Ark in pairs. The Ark became a huge barn for the animals and a safe houseboat for the believers.

The animals came running—
giraffes and rhinos, elephants
and camels, monkeys and
wolves, cats and kangaroos,
bears and horses, cows and
sheep, lions and tigers—
and all went into the Ark in pairs.

There were chickens and ducks, flamingos and hawks, peacocks and pelicans, ostriches and hens— to name but a few.

Birds both tiny and big that flew high above the earth came along too. All were gathered in pairs and led on board.

Tortoises, snails and turtles came crawling along the ground. Then came frogs and grasshoppers who hopped right into the Ark. Rabbits too ran races— let's see who gets on board first! And finally came the crocodiles with their big jaws.

No sooner had all the creatures come on board and the supplies had been stowed away, than black clouds began to cover the sky. First, there was a drizzle, then the rains came. More and more rain fell each day. Day after day, rain and more rain. The whole world seemed to be dark. It became darker and darker with strong winds blowing from every side and water rising in huge waves as far as the eye could see.

Allah commanded the floodgates of heaven to open and the ground to crack open so that a fountain of water came shooting up. The rivers overflowed and water fell in torrents. The Ark rose and fell on waves as tall as mountains. More and more water came till the valleys were filled, the trees were covered by the waters, the hills disappeared and the mountains themselves sank out of sight. The world was like an enormous sea— the only thing one could see was water everywhere. Far down below, all those who had paid no attention to the call of the Prophet Nuh ﷺ and remained on land were drowned in the mighty flood.

With the rain hammering on the roof and a great wind that roared all around, the Ark went on sailing amidst the waves. The thunder rolled and the lightning flashed from the angry skies. Everyone on board was very frightened, but Nuh ﷷ kept praying to his Lord for His Mercy at this great moment of trial.

When the flood had reached its peak, Allah commanded the earth to swallow up its water and sky to hold back the rain. The water began to dry up. The rain had stopped! The clouds began to part. As the level of the water began to go down, the mountain peaks began to rear up out of it. The Ark was caught by the peak of Mount Judi in a land now known as Turkey and rested upon it.

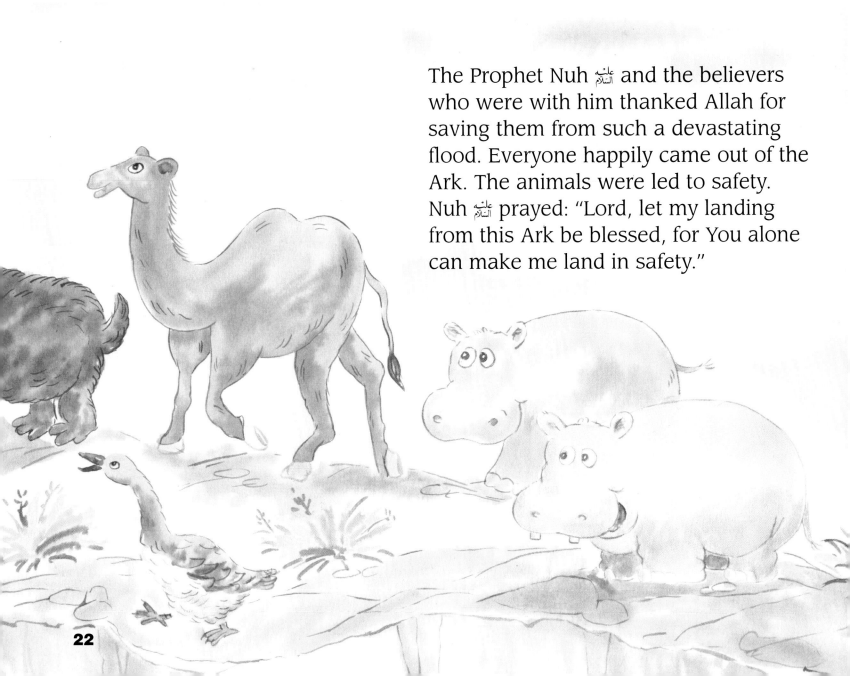

The Prophet Nuh ﷺ and the believers who were with him thanked Allah for saving them from such a devastating flood. Everyone happily came out of the Ark. The animals were led to safety. Nuh ﷺ prayed: "Lord, let my landing from this Ark be blessed, for You alone can make me land in safety."

In this way Allah made the flood and the Ark of Nuh ﷺ a sign and a warning for future generations.